BULLY'S

BULLSEYE™

QUIZ BOOK

SparkPool

Contents

Instructions

Players (either individually or in teams) specify which category they want to answer questions from (e.g. Music). They throw the dart at the board, aiming to get it into the Music section. If they succeed, they must correctly answer a question from the Music part of the book – and score however many points are shown in the segment that the dart has landed in. They then get another turn.

If they answer the question incorrectly, they get no points and another player/team takes their turn.

If they do not get the dart in the correct section (e.g. it lands in Geography instead), they can choose to answer a Geography question (and win the points) or pass. If they pass, they do not get to take another turn and another player/team takes their turn.

If they hit the Bullseye, they can answer a question from any topic of their choice.

Once a topic has been selected in this round and a question answered correctly, it cannot be chosen again (e.g. the next team can't also pick Music if points have already been won in that category).

Up to the oche – and listen to Tony!

TV & Film Quiz 1

1. Who is the youngest actor to win a Best Actor Oscar?

2. In which film did Johnny Depp only say 169 words?

3. Who did Ted Danson play in *Cheers*?

4. Which duo gave us the 'Four Candles' sketch?

5. Who directed *The Grand Budapest Hotel*?

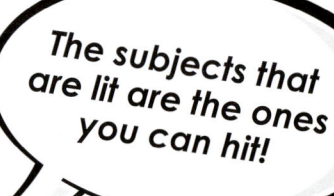

The subjects that are lit are the ones you can hit!

6. *I'm Always Here* was the theme tune to which TV series?

7. In *Eastenders*, what was the name of Robbie Jackson's dog?

8. Which film starred Sandra Bullock and Melissa McCarthy?

9. Who is older, Matt Damon or Ben Affleck?

10. Who won the first series of *The X Factor*?

TV & Film Quiz 2

1. What is *Strictly Come Dancing* known as in the USA?

2. Which channel first broadcast *The IT Crowd*?

3. Who played Howard Hughes in 2004 film, *The Aviator*?

Go for your lights.

4. In which country was actress Isla Fisher born?

5. What character did Jennifer Lawrence play in *The Hunger Games*?

6. Which 2009 film is the highest grossing film of all time (as of 2021)?

7. Which TV presenter was in a relationship with the brother of Kate Middleton?

8. Which Bill was a member of *The Goodies*?

9. Which cartoon character was framed in one of the biggest films of 1988?

10. Who played Betty in *Some Mothers Do 'Ave 'Em*?

TV & Film Quiz 3

1 Which actor played the roles of Granville and Del Boy?

2 What was the highest grossing film of 2009?

3 Which movie beat *Saving Private Ryan* to win Best Picture Oscar?

4 Who was the host of the ITV series *Odd One In*?

You've got the time it takes for the board to revolve...

5 Which 1982 film holds the record for the highest number of extras used?

6 Who played James Bond in *Die Another Day*?

7 Which silent movie won movie won the Best Picture Oscar in 2012?

8 What was ITV's version of Ceefax?

9 Who played Elsie Tanner in *Coronation Street*?

10 Who did Tim McInnerny play in *Blackadder Goes Forth*?

TV & Film Quiz 4

1 How many *Police Academy* films have been made, up to 2021?

2 In which year did *Deadwood* reach our screens?

Super, smashing, great.

3 Since 2014, each episode of the TV show *Deal or No Deal* starts with how many sealed boxes?

4 'Now, who would live in a house like this?' is the catchphrase on which TV show?

5 Who wrote *Trainspotting*?

6 Who played Antonio Salieri in the film *Amadeus*?

7 Who is Anton du Beke's professional dance partner?

8 *My Favorite Things* is a song from which musical?

9 What drink does Fredo ask for in *The Godfather Part II*?

10 What does 'a Mars a day' help you to do?

Music Quiz 1

1 What was Take That's big comeback hit in 2006?

2 Who released the album *Let Go* in 2003?

3 Which Rhianna song spent 10 weeks at number one in 2007?

4 Alex Turner is the lead singer of which band?

5 Who featured on Eminem's hit *Stan*?

6 What did JLS stand for?

7 Which band had a hit with *That's Not My Name*?

8 Who was known as the 'King of Skiffle'?

9 Who had a huge hit with *China in Your Hand*?

10 Scientist Dr Brian Cox was the keyboard player with which chart-topping 1990s band?

You win nothing but your BFH... Bus Fare Home.

Music Quiz 2

1. Who had the first new number one of the 1990s with *Hangin' Tough*?

2. Who wrote the song *Blue Moon*?

3. Which band had a minor hit with *James Dean*?

You've had a good night out – but you go home with nowt!

4. Which Bill was the producer of *Blood Brothers*?

5. Whose biggest hit was *He's on the Phone*?

6. Which singer spent more weeks in the UK single chart than any other in the 1980s?

7. Which Bowie song contains the line 'then I put him on a train to Eastbourne'?

8. What was the biggest hit for Muse in the UK?

9. What instrument was Acker Bilk famed for playing?

10. Who is the oldest Spice Girl?

Music Quiz 3

1. Who composed *The Nutcracker Suite*?

2. Who released the song *Who's Sorry Now* in 1957?

3. Which boxer appears on the cover of The Beatles' *Sgt. Pepper's Lonely Hearts Club Band* album?

4. Who were the two brothers in Oasis?

5. What song is traditionally sung by Scouts, Guides and Brownies around the campfire?

6. What was Elvis Presley's first *Billboard* pop chart number one?

7. Who was the last person to join The Rolling Stones?

8. *Sailing By* is a piece of music played before which BBC Radio 4 broadcast?

9. Which jazz musician was famous for *Take Five*?

10. Who sang the theme tune to the eighties sitcom *A Fine Romance*?

Non dart player to throw first...

Music Quiz 4

1. Who wrote the song *You Can Leave Your Hat On*?

2. The musical *Kiss Me Kate* is based on which Shakespeare play?

3. In which song did John Lennon set out to write the most confusing lyrics he could?

4. Which country is the birthplace of opera?

5. Which music duo met as children in Queens, NYC?

6. Who was the manager of The Beatles?

Let's check that with Bully.

7. What was the most famous song written by Francis Scott Lee?

8. How was Terence (Terry) Nelhams-Wright better known?

9. Who composed *La Bohème*?

10. In which year did Leonard Bernstein die?

Literature Quiz 1

1 What does the H. G. stand for in H. G. Wells?

2 Bertie Wooster and Flashman are both residents of which London square?

3 Who wrote *Alice's Adventures in Wonderland*?

4 Who is best known for writing *The Chronicles of Narnia*?

5 What is Shakespeare's shortest play?

Now the cash you won for charity earlier... that's safe.

6 Who has been the most translated author in the world since 1979?

7 Which book's opening line is: 'Hale knew, before he had been in Brighton three hours, that they meant to murder him'?

8 Whose first book was *The Mysterious Affair at Styles*?

9 Who wrote *Tom Jones*?

10 Who was Don Quixote's sidekick?

Literature Quiz 2

1. What is Jack Dawkins' nickname in *Oliver Twist*?

2. In which year was the first *Harry Potter* book released?

Up to the oche – and listen to Tony!

3. Mellors was the lover of which fictional character?

4. Whose biography was entitled *Long Walk to Freedom*?

5. What was the ill-received sequel to *To Kill a Mockingbird*?

6. Who wrote *Ulysses*?

7. Which English war poet died on the way to Gallipoli?

8. Who said: 'The true measure of a man is how he treats someone who can do him absolutely no good'?

9. Who wrote *Roots*?

10. Which poem gave us the line 'April is the cruellest month'?

Literature Quiz 3

1 Which American poet is often known as the 'Father of Free Verse'?

2 Who wrote *Glengarry Glen Ross*?

3 Who is best known for his book *Les Prophéties*?

4 How many books were in *The Hitchhiker's Guide to the Galaxy*?

5 What was the name of the fictional retreat in James Hilton's *Lost Horizon*?

6 The ghost of Banquo haunts which Shakespeare character?

7 Who wrote *The Prime of Miss Jean Brodie*?

8 Who wrote the novel *Our Mutual Friend*?

9 Who wrote *Rebecca*?

10 Who is the fictional character that Tom Sawyer was infatuated with?

Look at what you could have won.

Literature Quiz 4

1. R. D. Blackmore is most famous for writing which novel?

2. Which French novelist was the best-known practitioner of the literary school of naturalism?

3. Which famous playwright said 'Medicine is my lawful wife'?

Throwers and knowers.

4. What is Dr Watson's Christian name in the *Sherlock Holmes* stories?

5. Who was Shakespeare's wife?

6. Who wrote *Oranges Are Not the Only Fruit*?

7. How is the *Book of Columba* also known?

8. What famous maze is mentioned in *Three Men in a Boat*?

9. Who wrote *The Fall of the House of Usher*?

10. Which book is subtitled *The Modern Prometheus*?

Sport Quiz 1

1 What number did Lionel Messi wear when he played for FC Barcelona?

2 Who led England to their first Grand Slam in 23 years?

3 Who was appointed manager of Valencia CF in December 2015?

4 Who pioneered the backwards jump in high jump?

All for the throw of a dart!

5 How many players are in a rugby league team?

6 What is the name of the NFL team from Cincinnati?

7 How many players in a men's shinty team?

8 Which retired cricketer is sometimes referred to as GLY (Greatest Living Yorkshireman)?

9 A corner at Silverstone race track is named after which prestigious school?

10 What report recommended that all major stadia go to all-seater?

Sport Quiz 2

You've got the time it takes for the board to revolve...

1. In what city do Bohemian FC play?

2. What is the last event of a decathlon?

3. Manchester United paid £29 million for which Leeds player in 2002?

4. Peter Fleming was the doubles partner for many years of which tennis player?

5. In football, who are The Tigers?

6. Which company was the first to sponsor a one-day cricket tournament in the UK?

7. Which sport features nose diving and riding?

8. Which American football team plays in Baltimore?

9. Which Italian club is known as the Old Lady?

10. In horse racing, which of the British Classics is the longest-running?

Sport Quiz 3

1 In which sports would you find Michaela Tabb refereeing?

2 What nationality is the F1 driver Felipe Massa?

3 Which sport did Alan Shepard play on the moon?

4 At which winter sports resort is the Cresta Run?

Bully's bellowed you out there!

5 What is calculated to be the richest horse race in the world, as of 2021?

6 Who did Steffi Graf beat to win her first Wimbledon Singles title?

7 Which Grand Prix circuit is only 1.95 miles long?

8 In which sport is Tai Woffinden a champion?

9 In which martial art are bamboo swords used?

10 Where were the 1980 Summer Olympics held?

Sport Quiz 4

1. What is Tiger Woods' real first name?

2. Of what sport was Max Baer a top exponent?

3. In which sport is Daniel Purvis an Olympic medal winner?

4. In which sport is the Stanley Cup competed for?

5. What sport takes place on motorcycles that have only one gear and no brakes?

6. Which female British swimmer won two gold medals at the 2008 Summer Olympics?

7. Who invented basketball?

8. With which sport would you associate Edward Payson Weston?

9. Where was the Ryder Cup held in 2014?

10. Who is the only player, to date, to complete more than 30,000 runs in international cricket?

Remember, you can't beat a bit of Bully!

Politics Quiz 1

1 Who became Prime Minister at the age of 24?

2 'Make America Great Again' was the 2016 presidential election campaign of which candidate?

3 Who was made the Supreme Leader of North Korea in 2011?

4 What political tool involves a symbolic violation of the law?

And Bully's special prize...

5 How was The Dutch War of Independence also known?

6 What country was called The Gold Coast prior to its 1957 independence?

7 Who succeeded Kofi Annan as Secretary-General of the United Nations?

8 In what year did Chairman Mao die?

9 In which area of Cardiff does the Welsh Assembly sit?

10 Who was MP for Tatton, UK, before Martin Bell won the seat in 1997?

Politics Quiz 2

1. Who was elected leader of the Labour Party in the UK in 1980?

2. Who did the IRA murder on 27th November 1975?

Innnnnn one...

3. In what year was the Social Democratic Party formed?

4. What did Margaret Thatcher take away in 1971 when she was Secretary of State for Education and Science in Britain?

5. What was the name of the Italian ruling house after unification?

6. Who was chancellor of Germany from 1988 to 2005?

7. Who was the first Labour Prime Minister in the UK?

8. Who took over leadership of al-Qaeda after the death of Osama bin Laden?

9. Who preceded John Bercow as Speaker of the House of Commons?

10. Who did Russell Brand label a 'pound shop Enoch Powell'?

Politics Quiz 3

1 What is the name of the bell rung in Parliament to declare a vote is about to commence?

Go for your lights.

2 What socialist society was formed in 1884?

3 In the 1980s, where did women set up a blockade in protest of cruise missiles?

4 Who is the only US president to have resigned?

5 Which amendment to the US Constitution gave women the right to vote?

6 In which year did The Gambia achieve independence from Britain?

7 What name is given to the group made up of mostly senior politicians who advise the monarch?

8 How many times was William Gladstone Prime Minister?

9 Who was the first President of Zimbabwe?

10 Who was the UK Prime Minister at the outbreak of WWII?

Politics Quiz 4

1. Which political party was Anas Sarwar elected leader of in 2021?

2. What is the name of the official residence of the French president?

3. Who was the first president of Ireland?

4. Who was the first chancellor of the reunited Germany?

Let's check that with Bully.

5. Who was the first prime minister of free India?

6. In which year did Kenya win independence?

7. What empire existed from 1299 to 1922?

8. In which country was Boris Johnson born?

9. The House of Commons and The House of Lords meet in which palace?

10. Who was the leader of the Khmer Rouge regime?

History Quiz 1

1 What did J. M. W. stand for in the artist J. M. W. Turner?

2 What age was James Dean when he died?

3 In which year was eBay started?

101 or more for tonight's mystery star prize!

4 Who was the top pin-up girl for GIs during World War II?

5 In which year was The Orange Order founded?

6 Where was Queen Elizabeth II when her father died?

7 Who pulls the sovereign's coffin at a royal funeral?

8 Captain James Cook discovered which country in 1769 and claimed it for Great Britain?

9 In which year was Queen Elizabeth II born?

10 Which ancient Roman festival that began on 17th December had some of its customs absorbed into Christmas?

History Quiz 2

1. Which was the first US state to have a subway system?

2. Daniel Hooper is one of Britain's most famous environmental activists. How is he better known?

3. The Battle of Bosworth Field in 1485 was the last battle of which war?

4. In which modern country would the Hanging Gardens of Babylon be if they still existed?

5. In what year was the Boxing Day tsunami?

6. Elizabeth I was the last monarch of which royal house?

7. What was the original name of the City of Alexandria before it was renamed by Alexander the Great?

8. On what island did the dodo live?

9. In which year was the National Health Service (NHS) founded?

10. What did British Honduras become when it gained independence?

Stay out of the black and into the red, nothing in this game for two in a bed!

History Quiz 3

1. How did Mata Hari die?

2. Who would live in a cell attached to a church?

3. In which year did construction of the Berlin Wall begin?

4. Where did the Boxer Rebellion take place?

Mooooo!

5. In which year did the dot-com bubble burst?

6. What was the name of Churchill's Kent home?

7. In which year was the Empire State Building finished?

8. The Lion's Mound commemorates the site of which battle?

9. Levi Strauss is associated with the invention of which garment?

10. Who was the leader of the Bosnian Serbs during the Bosnian War?

History Quiz 4

1 In which year did Helen Sharman travel to space?

2 Who invented the bouncing bomb?

3 Who is the patron saint of Venice?

4 Bacchus was the Roman god of what drink?

5 Who designed the Cenotaph in Whitehall, London?

6 In which country was James Watt born?

7 First made in 1959, what type of transport was the SR.N1?

8 In Greek mythology, who was the Titan god of endurance and astronomy?

9 In what year was Rolihlahla (Nelson) Mandela released from prison?

10 Why was Felix Baumgartner in the news in 2012?

You've had a good night out – but you go home with nowt!

General Knowledge Quiz 1

1. What is the name of the container or room in which the bones of dead people are placed?

2. What does 'antebellum' mean?

3. Where is Lake Como?

Up to the oche – and listen to Tony!

4. What is a second full moon in a month called?

5. What was Beethoven's Christian name?

6. Which of the presidents on Mount Rushmore is wearing glasses?

7. How many nibbles in a byte?

8. What is a yurt?

9. What is the usual colour of copper sulphate?

10. What is the name of the drink made from fermented honey?

General Knowledge Quiz 2

1 Who wrote the original James Bond books?

2 What is the most southerly capital city in the world?

3 What company was founded by Richard Block and David Quayle?

4 Which famous retailer was founded in 1884 in Leeds?

Let's check that with Bully.

5 Who was Popeye's girlfriend?

6 What colour road did Dorothy follow?

7 What is the name of David Bowie's film director son?

8 Highclere Castle was the setting for ITV's *Downton Abbey*, in which county is it located?

9 The steel for Blackpool Tower was made in which northeast town?

10 How many possible first moves are there in chess?

General Knowledge Quiz 3

1. What is a group of pandas called?

2. Bronze is an alloy of which two metals?

3. What is Daltonism a form of?

Now the cash you won for charity earlier... that's safe.

4. How often does a census take place?

5. Who directed *Mulholland Drive*?

6. What is Tchaikovsky's ballet *Le Lac des Cygnes* commonly called?

7. What is the name of the brush in the sport of curling?

8. What was the name of Elvis Presley's Memphis mansion?

9. Kopi Luwak is a very expensive type of what drink?

10. What flavour is the liqueur Triple Sec?

General Knowledge Quiz 4

1. In which city is *A Midsummer Night's Dream* set?

2. What everyday product comes from the Aztec word for bitter water?

3. Which bell is synonymous with the name Lloyds of London?

4. If you have otalgia, what are you suffering from?

5. In nature, cocksfoot and Yorkshire fog are types of what?

Innnnnn one...

6. Which *Variations* brought lasting fame to Sir Edward Elgar?

7. Who wrote *The Waste Land*?

8. What date is St Swithin's Day?

9. In which game would you get a Double Top?

10. What name is given to the Japanese Mafia?

Science Quiz 1

1. What is the chemical symbol for table salt?

2. Which planet's moons include Miranda and Titania?

3. Of what is the ohm the standard measurement?

You've got the time it takes for the board to revolve...

4. Which chemical element has the atomic number 2?

5. In which country would you find the active volcano, Santorini?

6. A geyser is a spring characterised by intermittent discharge of water ejected turbulently by steam. Where is the original geyser from, which all others take their name?

7. Mycology is the study of what?

8. Named after an element, what was the name of the USA's first manned space programme?

9. How many orbits did Yuri Gagarin complete in Vostok I?

10. What is the name of the computer that picks out Premium Bond winners?

Science Quiz 2

1 Which gas is sometimes called marsh gas?

2 Dounreay Nuclear Power station was an FBR – what does 'FBR' stand for?

3 What acid is found in an ant bite?

4 What is the male part of a flower called?

5 Who invented the television?

Throwers and knowers.

6 How many bits in a byte?

7 With whom did Thomas Edison fight the War of the Currents?

8 Who invented logarithms?

9 Which family invented the whirlpool?

10 A dolorimeter is an instrument used to measure what?

Science Quiz 3

1 What letter is represented in Morse code by a single dot?

2 Agliophobia is the fear of what?

3 How many fluid ounces in a pint?

4 How many times bigger is A3 paper than A4?

5 How many squares on a Rubik's Cube?

All for the throw of a dart!

6 How many degrees are there in a right angle?

7 Phagophobia is the fear of what?

8 What is the study of insects called?

9 Iron pyrite is more commonly known as what?

10 What is the first element on the periodic table?

Science Quiz 4

1. What is the opposite of an acid?

2. Which element has the symbol Sn?

3. What colour flame does sulphur produce when burned?

4. How is nitrous oxide also known?

5. What is a neutral pH level?

Look at what you could have won.

6. Francis Crick and James Watson discovered the structure of what?

7. Who is known as the Father of Nuclear Physics?

8. What is the process of splitting atoms called?

9. Who discovered penicillin?

10. If something is stannic, which metal does it contain?

Geography Quiz 1

1 Which country administers Bora Bora?

2 What line on a map connects places of equal rainfall?

3 The name of which sea means 'middle earth'?

4 What type of cloud can form a tornado?

Go for your lights.

5 How many square feet in an acre?

6 What city was the capital of Australia from 1901 to 1927?

7 What is the first colour on the French flag before red and white?

8 In which country would you find the Po river?

9 What island is known as the Emerald Isle of the Caribbean?

10 On which specific island is Pearl Harbour located?

Geography Quiz 2

1. Which country is the largest producer of potassium?

2. What is the capital of Canada?

3. Where is the Great Bitter Lake?

4. Which country has the longest coastline?

5. What strait connects the Persian Gulf with the Arabian Sea?

Remember, you can't beat a bit of Bully!

6. What is Pleasant Island now known as?

7. What are states of Switzerland called?

8. What city is the capital of Qatar?

9. On which island will you find Fingal's Cave?

10. What is the name of the 73 miles constructed by the Romans across modern-day northern England?

Geography Quiz 3

1. Kilroot, an ancient salt mine, is located in which area of the UK?

2. What is the longest motorway in the UK?

3. What canal links the Atlantic and the Pacific?

The subjects that are lit are the ones you can hit!

4. What is the smallest country on mainland Africa?

5. To which South American country does Easter Island belong?

6. In which US state is Shenandoah National Park located?

7. What is the driest non-polar desert in the world?

8. Do penguins inhabit the North or South Pole?

9. Is a chinook wind warm or cold?

10. If you landed at Charles de Gaulle Airport, which city is it likely you'll be visiting?

Geography Quiz 4

1. The Santa Clara County is located in which US state?

2. Which continent is home to the tsetse fly?

3. Which desert makes up the majority of the territory in Botswana?

4. What is the second largest city in Egypt?

Bully's bellowed you out there!

5. What is the building at the centre of Islam's most sacred mosque, Al-Masjid al-Haram?

6. The ancient city of Tyre is now part of which modern country?

7. Where was the first new town in Britain?

8. Near which town does the River Ribble meet the sea?

9. The Great Barrier Reef lies off the coast of which Australian state?

10. In which body of water would you be if you were at 0 degrees longitude, 0 degrees latitude?

People Quiz 1

1. Who created *Tintin*?

2. Who won a record eight gold medals in the 2008 Summer Olympics in Beijing?

3. Who is Loretta Lynn's famous sister?

4. Who founded the Virgin Group?

5. What was David Bowie's real name?

Throwers and knowers.

6. Who created 'TheFacebook', a predecessor of social networking website Facebook?

7. Who was the manager of Oasis?

8. Who wrote *Cinderella*, *Little Red Riding Hood* and *The Sleeping Beauty*?

9. Who founded the Veritas political party?

10. Who was the leader of the Diversity dance troupe?

People Quiz 2

1. Who played Charlie Chaplin in the 1992 biopic?

2. Who narrates *Come Dine With Me*?

3. Who is Kate Hudson's mother?

4. Who was prime minister at the time of Princess Diana's death?

5. Who was president of Venezuela from 1999 to 2013?

6. Who gave voice to Shrek?

7. Who was born first, Miley Cyrus or Justin Bieber?

8. Who was the male presenter of *Total Wipeout*?

9. Who was the first pilot to break the sound barrier?

10. Who gave us the *Water Lilies* series of paintings?

Audience, what should they do?

People Quiz 3

1 Who is former Dr Who Peter Davison's son-in-law?

2 Who was George V's consort?

3 In which year did Diana Princess of Wales die?

4 Who shot Lee Harvey Oswald?

5 Who is known as The Naked Chef?

6 Who played Quentin Crisp in the TV film *The Naked Civil Servant*?

7 At what age did Rafael Nadal turn professional?

8 Who became the prime minister of India in 2014?

9 Who is Warren Beatty's older sister?

10 Who opened his circus, The Greatest Show on Earth, in Brooklyn in 1871?

People Quiz 4

1. Which composer appears as a character in *Gosford Park*?

2. Which Monty Python member directed *Brazil*?

3. What is the name of Alexander Armstrong's seated assistant on the game show *Pointless*?

4. Jeff Bezos was the founder of which multinational company?

5. How many children did Charlie Chaplin have?

Innnnnn one...

6. Who was the first Westerner to travel to the central portion of the Niger River?

7. What was Jackson Pollock's nickname?

8. Who is older, Robert De Niro or Al Pacino?

9. In which decade was Amy Winehouse born?

10. Who began presenting *Just a Minute* in 1967?

Answers

TV & Film Quiz 1

1 Adrien Brody
2 *Edward Scissorhands*
3 Sam Malone
4 The Two Ronnies
5 Wes Anderson
6 *Baywatch*
7 Wellard
8 *The Heat*
9 Matt Damon
10 Steve Brookstein

TV & Film Quiz 2

1 *Dancing with the Stars*
2 Channel 4
3 Leonardo DiCaprio
4 Oman
5 Katniss Everdeen
6 Avatar
7 Donna Air
8 Bill Oddie
9 Roger Rabbit
10 Michele Dotrice

TV & Film Quiz 3

1 Sir David Jason
2 *Avatar*
3 *Shakespeare in Love*
4 Bradley Walsh
5 *Gandhi*
6 Pierce Brosnan
7 *The Artist*
8 ORACLE
9 Pat Phoenix
10 Captain Kevin Darling

TV & Film Quiz 4

1 7
2 2004
3 23
4 *Through the Keyhole*
5 Irvine Welsh
6 F. Murray Abraham
7 Erin Boag
8 *The Sound of Music*
9 Banana daquiri
10 Work, rest and play

Music Quiz 1

1 *Patience*
2 Avril Lavigne
3 *Umbrella*
4 Arctic Monkeys
5 Dido
6 Jack the Lad Swing
7 The Ting Tings
8 Lonnie Donegan
9 T'Pau
10 D:Ream

Music Quiz 2

1 New Kids On The Block
2 Rodgers and Hart
3 Eagles
4 Bill Kenwright
5 Saint Etienne
6 Shakin' Stevens
7 *The Laughing Gnome*
8 *Supermassive Black Hole*
9 The clarinet
10 Geri Halliwell

Music Quiz 3

1 Tchaikovsky
2 Connie Francis
3 Sonny Liston
4 Noel and Liam Gallagher
5 *Ging Gang Goolie*
6 *Heartbreak Hotel*
7 Ronnie Wood
8 *The Shipping Forecast*
9 Dave Brubeck
10 Dame Judi Dench

Music Quiz 4

1 Randy Newman
2 *The Taming of the Shrew*
3 *I Am The Walrus*
4 Italy
5 Simon and Garfunkel
6 Brian Epstein
7 *The Star Spangled Banner*
8 Adam Faith
9 Giacomo Puccini
10 1990

Answers

Literature Quiz 1

1 Herbert George
2 Berkeley Square
3 Lewis Carroll
4 C. S. Lewis
5 *The Comedy of Errors*
6 Agatha Christie
7 *Brighton Rock*
8 Agatha Christie
9 Henry Fielding
10 Sancho Panza

Literature Quiz 2

1 The Artful Dodger
2 1997
3 Lady Chatterley
4 Nelson Mandela
5 *Go Set a Watchman*
6 James Joyce
7 Rupert Brooke
8 Samuel Johnson
9 Alex Haley
10 *The Waste Land*

Literature Quiz 3

1 Walt Whitman
2 David Mamet
3 Nostradamus
4 5
5 Shangri-La
6 Macbeth
7 Muriel Spark
8 Charles Dickens
9 Daphne du Maurier
10 Becky Thatcher

Literature Quiz 4

1 Lorna Doone
2 Émile Zola
3 Anton Chekhov
4 John
5 Anne Hathaway
6 Jeanette Winterson
7 *The Book of Kells*
8 Hampton Court Maze
9 Edgar Allan Poe
10 *Frankenstein*

Sport Quiz 1

1 10
2 Bill Beaumont
3 Gary Neville
4 Dick Fosbury
5 13
6 Cincinnati Bengals
7 12
8 Geoffrey Boycott
9 Stowe School
10 The Taylor Report

Sport Quiz 2

1 Dublin
2 1,500-metre run
3 Rio Ferdinand
4 John McEnroe
5 Hull City
6 Gillette
7 Surfing
8 The Baltimore Ravens
9 Juventus
10 The St Leger

Sport Quiz 3

1 Snooker and pool
2 Brazilian
3 Golf
4 St. Moritz
5 The Saudi Cup
6 Gabriela Sabatini
7 Monaco
8 Speedway
9 Kendo
10 Moscow

Sport Quiz 4

1 Eldrick
2 Boxing
3 Gymnastics
4 Ice hockey
5 Speedway
6 Rebecca Adlington
7 James Naismith
8 Pedestrianism
9 Gleneagles
10 Sachin Tendulkar

Answers

Politics Quiz 1

1. William Pitt the Younger
2. Donald Trump
3. Kim Jong-un
4. Civil disobedience
5. The Eighty Years' War
6. Ghana
7. Ban Ki Moon
8. 1976
9. Cardiff Bay
10. Neil Hamilton

Politics Quiz 2

1. Michael Foot
2. Ross McWhirter
3. 1981
4. Free school milk
5. House of Savoy
6. Gerhard Schröder
7. Ramsay MacDonald
8. Ayman al-Zawahiri
9. Michael Martin
10. Nigel Farage

Politics Quiz 3

1. A division bell
2. The Fabian Society
3. Greenham Common
4. Richard Nixon
5. The 19th Amendment
6. 1965
7. The Privy Council
8. 4
9. Canaan Banana
10. Neville Chamberlain

Politics Quiz 4

1. The Scottish Labour Party
2. The Élysée Palace
3. Douglas Hyde
4. Helmut Kohl
5. Jawaharlal Nehru
6. 1963
7. The Ottoman Empire
8. USA
9. Westminster
10. Pol Pot

History Quiz 1

1. Joseph Mallord William
2. 24
3. 1995
4. Rita Hayworth
5. 1795
6. Kenya
7. Royal Navy Sailors
8. New Zealand
9. 1926
10. Saturnalia

History Quiz 2

1. Boston
2. Swampy
3. Wars of the Roses
4. Iraq
5. 2004
6. Tudor
7. Rhacotis
8. Mauritius
9. 1948
10. Belize

History Quiz 3

1. Firing squad
2. An anchorite or anchoress
3. 1961
4. China
5. 2000
6. Chartwell
7. 1931
8. The Battle of Waterloo
9. Jeans
10. Radovan Karadžić

History Quiz 4

1. 1991
2. Barnes Wallis
3. San Mark
4. Wine
5. Sir Edwin Lutyens
6. Scotland
7. Hovercraft
8. Atlas
9. 1990
10. For the highest freefall

Answers

General Knowledge Quiz 1

1 An ossuary
2 Before the war
3 Italy
4 Blue moon
5 Ludwig
6 Theodore Roosevelt
7 2
8 Large round tent
9 Blue
10 Mead

General Knowledge Quiz 2

1 Ian Fleming
2 Wellington, New Zealand
3 B&Q
4 Marks and Spencer
5 Olive Oyl
6 Yellow
7 Duncan Jones
8 Hampshire
9 Consett
10 20

General Knowledge Quiz 3

1 An embarrassment
2 Tin and copper
3 Colour blindness
4 Every 10 years
5 David Lynch
6 Swan Lake
7 Curling brush or broom
8 Graceland
9 Coffee
10 Orange

General Knowledge Quiz 4

1 Athens
2 Chocolate
3 The Lutine bell
4 Earache
5 Grasses
6 The Enigma Variations
7 T. S. Eliot
8 15th July
9 Darts
10 Yakuza

Science Quiz 1

1 NaCl
2 Uranus
3 Electrical resistance
4 Helium
5 Greece
6 Iceland
7 Fungi
8 Project Mercury
9 1
10 ERNIE

Science Quiz 2

1 Methane
2 Fast breeder reactor
3 Formic acid
4 Stamen
5 John Logie Baird
6 8
7 Nikola Tesla
8 John Napier
9 The Jacuzzi family
10 Pain threshold

Science Quiz 3

1 E
2 Pain
3 20
4 Twice as big
5 54
6 90
7 Swallowing
8 Entomology
9 Fool's gold
10 Hydrogen

Science Quiz 4

1 An alkali
2 Tin
3 Blue
4 Laughing gas
5 7
6 DNA
7 Ernest Rutherford
8 Fission
9 Alexander Fleming
10 Tin

Answers

Geography Quiz 1

1 France
2 An isohyet
3 Mediterranean
4 Cumulonimbus
5 43560
6 Melbourne
7 Blue
8 Italy
9 Montserrat
10 Oahu

Geography Quiz 2

1 Canada
2 Ottawa
3 Egypt
4 Canada
5 The Strait of Hormuz
6 Nauru
7 Cantons
8 Doha
9 Staffa
10 Hadrian's Wall

Geography Quiz 3

1 Northern Ireland
2 The M6
3 The Panama Canal
4 The Gambia
5 Chile
6 Virginia
7 The Atacama Desert
8 The South Pole
9 Hot
10 Paris

Geography Quiz 4

1 California
2 Africa
3 The Kalahari Desert
4 Alexandria
5 The Kaaba
6 Lebanon
7 Stevenage
8 Lytham
9 Queensland
10 The Atlantic Ocean

People Quiz 1

1 Hergé
2 Michael Phelps
3 Crystal Gayle
4 Richard Branson
5 David Jones
6 Mark Zuckerberg
7 Alan McGee
8 Charles Perrault
9 Robert Kilroy-Silk
10 Ashley Banjo

People Quiz 2

1 Robert Downey Jr.
2 Dave Lamb
3 Goldie Hawn
4 Tony Blair
5 Hugo Chávez
6 Mike Myers
7 Miley Cyrus
8 Richard Hammond
9 Chuck Yeager
10 Monet

People Quiz 3

1 David Tennant
2 Mary of Teck
3 1997
4 Jack Ruby
5 Jamie Oliver
6 John Hurt
7 15
8 Narendra Modi
9 Shirley MacLaine
10 P. T. Barnum

People Quiz 4

1 Ivor Novello
2 Terry Gilliam
3 Richard Osman
4 Amazon
5 11
6 Mungo Park
7 Jack the Dripper
8 Al Pacino
9 The 1980s
10 Nicholas Parsons